GET INTO ART

STORIES

SUSIE BROOKS

KINGFISHER

KINGFISHER

First published 2015 by Kingfisher
an imprint of Macmillan Children's Books
a division of Macmillan Publishers Limited
20 New Wharf Road, London N1 9RR
Basingstoke and Oxford
Associated companies throughout the world
www.panmacmillan.com

Edited by Catherine Brereton and Polly Goodman
Designed by Peter Clayman
Cover design by Peter Clayman and Jane Tassie
Project photography by Peter Clayman
Picture research by AME Picture Research

ISBN 978 0 7534 3742 1

9 8 7 6 5 4 3 2 1
1TR/1114/LFG/UG/140MA
A CIP catalogue record for this book is available from the British Library.
Printed in China

CONTENTS

PICTURE A STORY

What's your favourite story? The chances are you have a picture of it in your mind!
Lots of artists choose stories as their subjects, from imaginary tales to historical events or things that have happened in people's lives. Children's books are packed with illustrations, while other works of art show stories in a single scene. It's true that every picture tells a story in its own individual way!

See how stories have inspired famous artists – then **let them inspire you too!** Each page of this book will tell you about a work of art and the person who created it. When you lift the flap, you'll find a project based on the artwork. Don't feel you have to copy it exactly. Half the fun of art is exploring your own ideas!

GETTING STARTED

There's a checklist on page 31 that will tell you what you need for each project, but it's a good idea to read through the steps before you begin. There are also some handy tips on the next page…

Always have a **pencil** and **rubber** handy. Making a rough **sketch** can help you plan a project and see how it's going to look.

PICK YOUR PAINT...

Acrylic paints are thick and bright – they're great for strong colours, or textures like grass.

Ready-mix paints are cheaper than acrylics but still bright. Use them when you need lots of paint.

Watercolours give a thinner colouring that you can build up in layers, called washes.

Use a mixture of thick and thin **paintbrushes**. Have a jam jar or plastic cup of water ready to rinse them in and a **palette** or paper plate for mixing paint.

acrylic paint

Lay some newspaper on your surface before you start to paint!

watercolour paint

sponged paint

TRY PASTELS...

Oil pastels have a bright, waxy look, like crayons. **Soft pastels** can be smudged and blended like chalk.

oil pastels

soft pastels

For painting, use thick **cartridge** or **watercolour paper** – anything too thin will wrinkle. **Pastel paper** has a rough surface that holds onto the colour.

Collect a range of **coloured papers and card** for collage and 3-D models.

Ready to start?
Let's **get into art!**

Look around at home for other art materials. Useful things include sponges, rags or cloths, scissors, string, glue, old packaging, drinking straws, felt or fabric and kitchen foil.

WILLIAM THE CONQUEROR'S FLEET

Bayeux Tapestry 11th century

Imagine a cartoon strip that's nearly the length of three swimming pools!
That's one way to describe the Bayeux Tapestry, which this sailing scene is a part of.

Sewn story

If you saw the whole Bayeux Tapestry, it might take you a while to find this boat – you'd have to search 70 metres of cloth decorated with 632 people, 202 horses, 560 other creatures, 41 ships and lots more! The pictures tell the story of William the Conqueror and his invasion of England over 900 years ago.

This scene shows William's fleet crossing the English Channel from Normandy, in France. They're on their way to victory at the Battle of Hastings. We can see the sails billowing on their wooden longboats, laden with horses, soldiers and shields. Every tiny detail is sewn in wool on linen fabric. In fact this type of stitching isn't called tapestry at all, but embroidery!

WHY WAS IT MADE?

The story on the Bayeux Tapestry is told from the invaders' point of view, so it was probably made as a celebration. We think that it was ordered by William's half brother, Bishop Odo of Bayeux. No one really knows who sewed it, but it might have been a group of nuns who were skilled at needlework.

HOMAGE TO BLÉRIOT

Robert Delaunay 1914

In 1909, an exciting story hit the news – someone had flown a plane across the English Channel! A few years later, Robert Delaunay celebrated it on canvas.

Soaring shapes

Flying a plane from France to England might not be a big deal today – but Louis Blériot was the first person to do it! He won a prize of £1000 and became a hero on both sides of the Channel. Delaunay chose a rainbow of flight-inspired shapes to honour him.

Look at the circles – do they remind you of spinning propellers? There's a biplane soaring above the Eiffel Tower, but Blériot flew a monoplane with only one set of wings. Can you see it here? Delaunay didn't want to create a detailed, realistic scene. Instead he painted bright, simple shapes that seem to whirl and flicker. They make us feel the energy and thrill of flying through the air!

WHO WAS DELAUNAY?

Robert Delaunay was born in France in 1885. He worked as a theatre designer before becoming a painter. As an artist he was inspired by different modern styles, from Impressionism to Cubism and Expressionism. He blended them in his own colourful world of bold, often abstract, shapes.

SCENE FROM
CINDERELLA

Arthur Rackham 1919

You might recognize this scene from the fairy tale *Cinderella*. Rackham brings the famous story to life with his simple but magical illustrations.

Telling tails

Can you tell what's happening here? The fairy godmother is turning six lizards into footmen! We can see them changing bit by bit from animal to human – look at their tails getting shorter. They'll soon be ready to take Cinderella to the ball in her pumpkin carriage.

Of course *Cinderella* is a made-up story, so no one really knows what the fairy godmother looked like. Rackham imagined her as a friendly, witchy character with a hooked nose and a pointy hat! He illustrated this scene and the rest of the book in a style called silhouette. He was brilliant at showing poses and expressions through plain black shapes with very little detail within them.

WHO WAS RACKHAM?

Arthur Rackham was born in England in 1867. He grew up loving drawing, and later made his name as a great illustrator. Known for his imaginative characters and enchanted scenes, he decorated the pages of many famous books – from children's fairy tales to Shakespeare plays!

AUTOMAT

Edward Hopper 1927

Some stories are imagined – and some make us do the imagining! In this painting, Hopper sets the scene for a story but leaves a sense of mystery dangling over it.

Puzzling picture

The painting makes us ask lots of questions. Who is this woman? What is she doing here? Is she waiting for someone? What sort of mood is she in? She is well dressed and wearing make-up. Is she on her way to or from work, or a party? Her clothes suggest that it's cold outside, but we can't tell from the dark sky whether it is early morning or night.

How long do you think the woman has been here for? She's still wearing a glove, so perhaps she has only recently sat down. But we can also see an empty plate in front of her – has she had time for something to eat? Maybe she is thinking about leaving. There's no action to give away the full story. Hopper leaves it up to us to fill in the gaps!

WHO WAS HOPPER?

Edward Hopper was born in the USA in 1882. He studied art and worked briefly as an illustrator before making his name as a painter. Hopper became famous for his quiet city scenes, with isolated figures and dramatic lighting. Most of the women he painted were modelled on his wife.

NOAH'S ARK

Canterbury Cathedral 13th century

Windows aren't just for looking out of – sometimes they tell stories instead! This one, made of colourful stained glass, illustrates a scene from the Bible.

Seeing the light

The man we can see here is Noah. In the Bible story, he builds a giant ark to save his family and two of every type of animal from a terrible flood. One day he sends out a dove, which returns with an olive branch in its beak. This tells Noah that the flood is dying down and land is somewhere within reach.

Imagine this picture as part of a huge cathedral window, packed with religious scenes. It was made at a time when few people were able to read, but they could learn a lot from the bright stained-glass images. As the sun moved around throughout the day, different windows would come alive like a coloured light show. It must have been exciting long before film or television were invented!

Stained glass is still used as an art form to tell stories, celebrate people's lives or events or just decorate rooms with dancing patterns of light. You can see windows like this in churches, mosques, synagogues and many other buildings – some people even have them in their homes! The way stained glass is made has hardly changed since it was invented, though many more colours are available today.

HOW WAS IT MADE?

To stain glass, it had to be melted and coloured with chemicals, before cooling and flattening out. Small details, such as faces and feathers, were painted on – often with a black pigment mixed with urine! The pieces were carefully cut to shape, then arranged and joined together with strips of lead.

THE SPINNERS

Diego Velázquez, *about* 1657

This impressive painting tells a story in two parts. It begins in the foreground, close to the viewer, then continues at the back of the scene.

Weaving a tale

Velázquez chose a Greek myth, the Fable of Arachne, as the subject of his painting. It tells of a peasant girl called Arachne who challenged the goddess Athena to a weaving contest. When Arachne produced a tapestry as brilliant as Athena's, the goddess became angry – and turned the poor girl into a spider!

Athena is the figure in the headscarf, while Arachne has her back to us on the right. They are busy spinning yarn for their work. Velázquez arranged them carefully, leading our eye slowly towards the lit-up back room where Arachne's finished tapestry hangs on the wall. We can see Athena in a helmet in front of it, raising her arm in fury. Velázquez expects us to know what happens next!

WHO WAS VELÁZQUEZ?

Diego Velázquez was born in Spain in 1599. At the age of 11, he became apprenticed to a local painter who recognized his talent at art. Later, he was made court painter to King Philip IV and lived in the royal palace. He also travelled to Italy, where other great artists influenced his work.

LONE DOG'S WINTER COUNT

Lone Dog 1800–1870

Here's a story that you read from the inside out!

Each symbol in this spiral represents a year in the life of the Native American Yanktonai Nakota people.

Dates to remember

We may use dates in our diaries, but Lone Dog and others used pictures instead. Every year they chose the most memorable thing that had happened and drew a symbol, or pictogram, for it. This built up a decorative record of their history – there are 70 years shown here.

Try and find the following: a spotty figure (many people died of smallpox), a lasso (wild horses were caught), two hands about to shake (a peace agreement), a black sun (solar eclipse). Other events include trading with Europeans, battles with other tribes, floods, pony thefts and a meteor shower. They're all drawn on a buffalo skin, or hide.

WHY A WINTER COUNT?

It's called a winter count because the Nakota measured their years between each first snowfall. Every year the elders met to decide on the event to record. As time passed, the keeper of the count had to remember what his symbols meant so he could tell the stories to others!

THE ARMADA PORTRAIT

Probably George Gower, *about* 1588

Every person has a story – and Elizabeth I of England's was an impressive one! This painting is more than just a portrait of the powerful and popular queen.

Glory story

In the year this picture was painted, the British defeated an invasion from Spain, known as the Spanish Armada. We can see two scenes from the battle in the background, to either side of the queen. Under her hand is a globe, a symbol of the power that she held in the world. Her clothes and jewels tell us that she was rich and grand.

In fact, this visual story has a few fibs in it too. In 1588, Elizabeth was 55 years old with wrinkled skin, black teeth, narrow lips and thinning hair! This wasn't the image she wanted people to remember, so she ordered the artist to show her as an ageless beauty, surrounded by wealth and glory.

WHO WAS GOWER?

This picture isn't signed by George Gower, but it seems likely that he painted it. Born in England in around 1540, he was Serjeant Painter to Queen Elizabeth from 1581. His main job was to create portraits of the royals, but he also painted decoration on their furniture, palaces and carriages.

ICARUS

Henri Matisse 1943

Sometimes stories can be told in the simplest of pictures! Matisse illustrated this mythological tale using just a few colours and shapes.

Forever falling

It's never a good idea to fly close to the sun when you're wearing wings made of feathers and wax! Icarus, a character from Greek mythology, found out the hard way when his home-made wings melted, sending him plummeting into the sea.

In Matisse's picture we see Icarus falling, his head tilted as if he's looking down below. The brilliant blue sky is filled with flashes of yellow that remind us of blazing sunlight. Icarus was an adventurer, and his brave heart glows red in his chest. The simple shapes and curves make the fall seem graceful, like a dance – but the heavy black of the figure suggests that this will not end well.

When Matisse created this picture, he was old and unwell, and his eyesight was failing. He worked by painting large sheets of paper and then cutting them into shapes – a method he called 'drawing with scissors'. In 1947, Matisse published a book called *Jazz* that was full of these colourful cut-outs. On some of the pages he included handwritten notes and thoughts.

WHO WAS MATISSE?

Matisse was born in France in 1869. He trained as a lawyer, but at the age of 20 he fell ill with appendicitis. His mother gave him a paintbox to help him pass the time, and that's when his love of art began. Matisse became very famous, creating paintings, drawings, prints, collages and sculptures. Some of his works have sold for over US $30 million!

WORLD UPSIDE DOWN

Jan Steen, *about* 1665

The world isn't actually upside down in this painting – but it isn't quite how it should be. Steen has woven in all sorts of little stories that tip ordinary life on its head!

Rowdy room

What do you see when you look at this household? Is there anything that seems a bit strange? Maybe it's the boy smoking a pipe, the lady asleep at the table or the dog tucking into her dinner! No one seems to notice the baby throwing her food and playing with an expensive necklace. There's an indoor pig, a duck on a guest and a monkey fiddling with a clock!

Jan Steen had a sense of humour. He loved to make jokes about the ordered lifestyles of people in the villages around him. While other Dutch artists painted prim and proper families in well-kept homes, Steen showed children with grown-up bad habits, and adults larking around like kids!

WHO WAS STEEN?

Jan Steen was born in Holland in 1625/26. His family were brewers and his paintings told stories of the everyday life around him. Often he included witty proverbs, or messages, in his work. *World Upside Down* is also known as *Beware of Luxury* – a warning about the penalties of being rich!

THE BATTLE
OF SAN ROMANO

Paolo Uccello, *about* 1438–40

The good thing about painting a battle story is you can pick the bits you show!

Uccello chose glory over gory in this enormous picture, painted for a family on the winning side.

A beautiful battle

In real life, Uccello's painting is three metres wide! It tells the story of a battle between the Italian cities of Florence and Sienna. Can you guess who is leading the victorious Florentine side? Of course it's the man on the white horse! He's Niccolò da Tolentino and he's the first thing we notice in the scene.

Uccello has ignored a lot of the reality of battle. His hero doesn't even wear a helmet to protect his head. Instead we see decorative costumes, beautiful scenery and a criss-cross pattern of scattered swords. Uccello had just discovered the technique of perspective, which gave his painting a 3-D feel. Apparently he would stay up all night trying to get the angles exactly right!

WHO WAS UCCELLO?

Paolo di Dono was born in Italy in 1397 (Uccello was really a nickname, given for his love of painting birds). He became apprenticed to a sculptor at the age of ten, then turned to painting in his teens. This picture, one of three he made of the same battle, is one of his most famous works.

DREAM OF A SUNDAY AFTERNOON IN ALAMEDA CENTRAL PARK

Diego Rivera 1947

Sometimes the strangest stories happen in our dreams! In this dream-like painting, Rivera takes a walk in the park with hundreds of characters from history.

Distant memories

The boy in striped socks is the artist himself, aged 10, with a frog and snake in his pockets. He holds hands with a living skeleton lady, dressed in a fancy plumed hat. Skeleton characters were a speciality of the artist José Guadalupe Posada, who stands on her other side. Behind the young Rivera we can also see Frida Kahlo, his future wife.

This is just a section of Rivera's huge picture, which he painted on a hotel wall. He mixed his own memories with the story of his home country, Mexico. While some scenes seem like the stuff of nightmares, the hot-air balloon is a symbol of hope. It's decorated with the national flag and RM for *República Mexicana*.

WHO WAS RIVERA?

Diego Rivera was born in Mexico in 1886. Even as a boy he loved drawing on walls, so no wonder he became famous for his murals! Rivera liked to paint scenes with a message, which often shocked other people. He created huge public pictures so that everyone could see what he believed in.

ART WORDS AND INFO

abstract Not representing an actual object, place or living thing. Abstract art often focuses on simplified shapes, lines, colours, or use of space.

apprentice Someone who works for an employer in order to learn a certain skill.

canvas A strong type of fabric that artists can paint or sew designs on.

collage A picture made by sticking bits of paper, fabric or other objects onto a surface.

court painter An artist who painted for a royal or noble family, often agreeing not to take on other work.

Cubism (1907–1920s) An art style that involved making images using simple geometric shapes.

embroidery The art of decorating fabric with stitched designs in wool or thread.

Expressionism (1905–1920s) An art style that was about feelings and emotions, often shown through distorted shapes or colours.

foreground The part of a picture or scene that appears nearest to the viewer.

illustrator An artist who creates illustrations – pictures that explain or decorate a story or other piece of writing.

Impressionism (1870s–1890s) An art style that focused on colour and the changing effects of light. Impressionist artists often painted outdoors and tried to capture passing moments.

landscape A scene or painting of a scene, usually in the countryside.

mural A picture painted on a wall.

mythological Relating to myths – traditional stories told by ancient cultures such as the ancient Greeks.

COLOUR CONNECTIONS

In art there are three primary colours – **red**, **yellow** and **blue**. These are colours that can't be mixed from any others. Each primary colour has an opposite, or complementary, which is made by mixing the other two.

If you mix a colour with its complementary, you'll get a shade of brown.

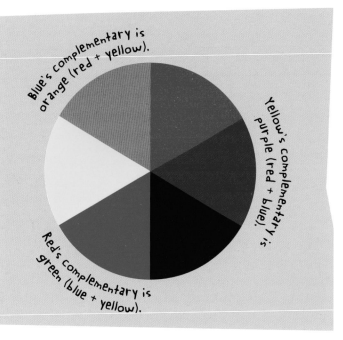

Blue's complementary is orange (red + yellow).

Yellow's complementary is purple (red + blue).

Red's complementary is green (blue + yellow).

perspective The art of showing three-dimensional objects on a flat page, creating the effect of depth or distance.

portrait A painting, sculpture or other artwork that shows an image of a particular person.

print A way of transferring an image from one surface to another. Prints are often made by spreading ink over a raised or engraved design, then pressing it onto paper. This makes a reverse image that can be reproduced many times.

proverb A short, popular saying that contains a message or piece of advice.

sculptor An artist who makes three-dimensional art, called sculpture. Carving and clay modelling are types of sculpture.

Serjeant Painter A highly honoured artist employed by a royal household.

silhouette A picture of something that shows the shape and outline only, usually coloured in black.

sketch A rough drawing or painting, often made to help plan a final artwork.

symbol A shape or icon that stands for, or represents, something else.

tapestry The art of weaving designs in wool or thread onto a stiff cloth or canvas.

texture The feel of a surface, such as rough brick or smooth glass.

three-dimensional (3-D) Describes something that has height, width and depth.

PROJECT CHECKLIST

Below is a list of materials you'll need for each project in this book. The ones in brackets are useful but you can manage without!

Sew a boat (page 7) colourful felt or other strong fabric, scissors, different coloured wool, large needle, glue

Salute to space (page 9) thick white paper, pencil, rubber, round objects or pair of compasses, oil pastels or wax crayons, watercolour paint, paintbrush, (cloth)

Character cut-outs (page 11) rough paper, pen or pencil, scissors, black paper, white pencil, glue, white paper, (coloured paper)

Secret story (page 13) coloured pastel paper, pencil, rubber, soft pastels

Window wings (page 15) A4 or A3 black paper, white pencil or crayon, scissors, coloured tissue paper, glue, sticky tack

Spinning spiders (page 17) stiff cardboard, pen or pencil, thick string or cord, scissors, strong craft glue, white paint, paper plate, coloured paper, black paint, black felt pen or marker

What counts? (page 19) thick white paper, tea bags, pencil, felt pens, crayons or paints and paintbrush

Fancy dressing (page 21) coloured paper, scissors, glue, paints, paper plate or palette, pencil, pen lid or bottle top, leaves, strip of cardboard, potato, onion or cabbage, foil, (gems or sequins)

Flying without wings (page 23) coloured card, pencil, scissors, thread, needle, sticky tape

Silly street (page 25) drawing paper, pencil, rubber, coloured paper, scissors, glue, old magazines, scraps of patterned paper

Battle in a box (page 27) large shoe box, paper, scissors, paints, paintbrush, glue, thin cardboard, (wool, feathers, drinking straws, shiny paper)

Up and away! (page 29) air-dry modelling clay, paintbrush, pencil, acrylic or ready-mix paints, string, scissors

INDEX